How to Be Courageous, Confident, and Consistent

Bee Devotionals By Sheila Textor

Copyright © 2023 by Sheila Textor, Bee Ministries.
All rights reserved. No part of this book may be reproduced, transmitted, or distributed in any form or by electronic means without prior written permission of the publisher, except in the form of short quotations for book reviews and certain other noncommercial uses permitted by copyright law.

Independently published by Bee Ministries.
Blytheville, Arkansas

ISBN: 978-1-7361575-9-6

All scriptures used in this devotional come from the King James Version of the Bible, which exists in the public domain in the United States.

Interior art designed for Bee Ministries by Victoria Neal @victorianeal2001.

Check out Sheila's other works on Amazon:
Life After the Mistake
How to Bee Prosperous
How to Be Intentional With Your Words
How to Be Healthy, Wealthy, and Wise
How to Be Prayerful, Powerful, and Purposeful
How to Believe in Your Dreams
ebook: *How to Be a Writer*

Find Sheila on YouTube at Bee Ministries
Facebook @LifeAfterTheMistake

How to Be Courageous, Confident, and Consistent

By Sheila Textor

Contents

Day 1 8
Day 2 12
Day 3 16
Day 4 20
Day 5 24
Day 6 28
Day 7 32
Day 8 36
Day 9 40
Day 10 44
Day 11 50
Day 12 54
Day 13 58
Day 14 62
Day 15 66
Day 16 70
Day 17 74
Day 18 78
Day 19 82
Day 20 86
Day 21 92
Day 22 96
Day 23 100
Day 24 104
Day 25 108
Day 26 112
Day 27 116
Day 28 120
Day 29 124
Day 30 128
Day 31 132
Why bees? 136

Introduction

There is no reason we can't be courageous, confident, and consistent in our daily walk with God. You will find each one of these actions in stories and promptings throughout the Bible. Even though courageous is the first action, consistency will be the key behind the other two. Consistency in any area will bring about confidence in whatever you are endeavoring to accomplish. The more you grow in an area, gaining confidence through consistency and practice, the more courageous you will become. God commands Joshua to be courageous. For God to choose Joshua to be Moses successor he had to have been consistent in following his leader. No doubt he showed confidence and courage to step up in that position. When we read the Bible we need to realize that it is our example. If it made it into the most read book in the world then it is definitely something we need to learn.

    Be consistent in your prayer time. Be consistent reading the Bible. Don't let it intimidate you. There are many ways to get the Word in your heart. You have to choose what works for you. I've never been one to set a yearly reading plan. I listen to hours of teaching, preaching and Bible studies. When I hear something that pricks my heart or causes me to pay attention I will look up those scriptures and let God minister to me.

    The more knowledgeable you are of the Word, the more confidence you will have. I am a very confident person. Some will scoff at you, but don't be moved by their insecurities. My confidence comes from meditating night and day in the Word. My flesh is weak, but I don't let my flesh rule me. As your confidence grows, so will your courage.

We know the Mark Twain saying, "Courage is not the absence of fear. It is acting in spite of it." We need a healthy fear. The world as we once knew it no longer exists. The days of traveling by ourselves or morning walks no longer feel safe. We can't allow the enemy to reign over us with fear mongering. He will drive us into isolation. Then he begins to attack weak areas in our lives. This courage that comes from God comes through the Spirit. The courage to write that book, to write that song, to start that business. The courage to step up and lead others. The courage to speak into people's lives and change the direction they are headed. We need courage to walk out the calling that God has placed on our life. God says in the Word be strong and of good courage.

PART 1: COURAGEOUS

Day 1

Have not I commanded thee? Be strong and of a good courage; be not afraid, neither be thou dismayed: for the L ORD thy God is with thee whithersoever thou goest.

Joshua 1:9

God didn't suggest Joshua be courageous, He commanded him. I don't believe it was a commandment like the Ten Commandments. It was more like an encouragement statement. Most are familiar with this story of Joshua being chosen by God way before Moses stepped off the scene. He had been a shadow to Moses. Joshua was with Moses when they crossed the Red Sea. He followed the fire by night and the cloud by day. He ate the manna from heaven. He defeated the Amaleks while Aaron and Hur held up Moses' hands. See the pattern. Joshua was being groomed to be the next leader. It was God's plan. When you feel like you're coming in second place, or when it seems that you are watching battles being won from a distance, just know that God is getting you ready to be the next leader, the next pastor, the next Sunday School teacher, the next choir leader. Most will already know what their next is, or what they want it to be. Let me gently nudge you in this devotional today to be strong and courageous. We have a lifetime of watching other courageous people walking out the calling of God in their lives. God entreats you to

Bee Courageous!

Prayer (speak aloud)

God, You are so faithful to not leave me clueless. You have sent others before me to fight the good fight of faith. Thank You for giving me all the stories in the Bible about courageous men and women that obeyed Your instructions. Some fought bears and lions, some fought the critics in their hometowns, some spoke with authority and cast out demons in the name of Jesus. Courage is definitely at the top of Your list. Even in my own life I have had courageous men and women leading by example. Thank You for speaking to me through Your Word and instructing me on how to be courageous. Amen.

Do you fear stepping out into unknown territory? Write about a time you moved ahead without all the details, but felt the courage to keep going.

Day 2

12 And the angel of the LORD **appeared unto him, and said unto him, The L**ORD **is with thee, thou mighty man of valour.
14 And the L**ORD **looked upon him, and said, Go in this thy might, and thou shalt save Israel from the hand of the Midianites: have not I sent thee?**

Judges 6:12, 14

This story is clearly not Joshua and Moses. We can tell by the way Gideon responds he doesn't have the courage he needs to fulfill this assignment. In verse 13, Gideon questions, wondering if God has forsaken them. Gideon didn't have Moses leading him. Gideon began to make excuses of why the angel surely had the wrong man. He uses his place in life to try to discount his assignment, saying he's from a small family. He just couldn't grasp that he had been chosen to be over this battle. They had been praying for God to send someone to help them. We all do that sometimes, we are looking for God to send help. We can't see ourselves as the help. We can sympathize with Gideon. He began to list all the reasons he wasn't qualified to do this great feat. His family was poor. He was the least in his father's house. I feel his insecurity, don't you? But there's a difference between insecurity and humility. We never want to come off as if we know we are the one God needs to pick. The posture of the heart matters. We need to be willing to say, "here am I send me," but with an attitude of total dependence on God to be with us. Gideon did rise up to meet the challenge and gained the courage he needed through God. God in His patience and care for Gideon, through signs and instructions, made sure the battle was won.

Prayer (speak aloud)

Here am I, Lord, send me. I will move forward in this world below as long as You promise to go with me. God, I am like Gideon sometimes when You come to me with an assignment. I make excuses for not moving immediately: My funds are low, things are tight, I don't know a lot about that. I must remember that You are not asking me to do something I can't. You won't guide me without providing for me. If I stay close to Thee, if I keep Your Word hidden in my heart I will be able to have the God-courage I need. Amen.

**What are some of your reasons for not moving out in a particular area when you feel God nudging you?
Do you desire to do something in the Kingdom?
What is stopping you?**

Day 3

16 And Ruth said, Intreat me not to leave thee, or to return from following after thee: for whither thou goest, I will go; and where thou lodgest, I will lodge: thy people shall be my people, and thy God my God:
17 Where thou diest, will I die, and there will I be buried: the LORD do so to me, and more also, if ought but death part thee and me.

Ruth 1:16–17

The story of Ruth is laced with courage. It's a story of uncertainty. It's a story of tragedy and triumph. Very few people leave their homeland to follow their in-laws after the death of a spouse. We love them, we are part of them, but most also have their own family that they were born into. Ruth was following her mother-in-law into a land that didn't really associate with her race. She was originally a Moabite, a people who were seen as cruel and generally not well-liked. Ruth was like Cinderella without the magic or the fairy tail. Ruth would go and work in the fields knowing that she was not like them. She knew that they could put her out of those fields. I could see why she would want better, she wanted to move on from where she was. Somehow she built up her courage through all the past hurts and took a chance at making a better life for herself. Through this great move of courage she became the wife of Boaz (a wealthy kinsman) and later the great-grandmother of David. How about you? Do you want to move on? Do you desire the courage Ruth had? My sweet friend you can attain this great courage by putting your trust in the God Naomi was returning to.

Prayer (speak aloud)

Thank You, God, for the courage to follow You even when things seem uncertain. Thank You for rewarding me with good when I take the necessary steps to move forward. Fear lurks at every corner. It screams, 'Don't move!' It rears its ugly head when there are decisions to be made. Fear of the unknown keeps me bound sometimes. God, You are the light in my path, the lamp unto my feet. I could not have this courage without You. Through You I can be a Ruth in my day. A courageous Christian fulfilling my purpose here on earth. Amen.

What do you like most about the story of Ruth? Can you see yourself in her story?

Day 4

And it was so, when the king saw Esther the queen standing in the court, that she obtained favour in his sight: and the king held out to Esther the golden sceptre that was in his hand. So Esther drew near, and touched the top of the sceptre.

Esther 5:2

It's hard to choose which verse to use for the story of Esther. I chose this one because this is the place where she could have died. No doubt it took a lot of courage to take this kind of stand for her people. Esther, like Ruth, played a very significant role in the lives of other people. I encourage all my readers to go read these stories in their settings. Esther was young but chosen. I love the fact that a whole book was named after her. She replaced another queen. She could not approach the king without being summoned. Her people were facing annihilation by an evil man named Haman, who served the king. Her uncle, Mordecai, who helped her get in this position as queen, reminded Esther she was there for such a time as this. She tells Mordecai to have their people, the Jews, fast for three days and she and her maidens would fast likewise. Then she would go to the king and if she perished, she perished. That my friend is courage on a whole different level. We see that the king was pleased to accept her request. Through her bravery she saved the Jews that day, and Haman got found out as an evil man. Even though her life was at stake, Esther had courage.

Prayer (speak aloud)

God, I thank You for the Ruths and the Esthers. Thank You for having these stories pinned in your Holy Word. I know that I am here for such a time as this. I will be strong and courageous. I will light my candle and run to the darkness. My family needs me to go to the King and ask for their lives. To be willing to be ridiculed for standing up against the enemy's tactics. I cancel every plot, plan, and scheme that Satan has prepared for my children and grandchildren. I call angel armies to assist me and fight the spirit of suicide. The spirits of oppression and depression. I am your courageous warrior. I am your Esther. Amen.

**Do you think you could do what Esther did?
How can you be the Esther for such a time as this?**

Day 5

Then said David to the Philistine, Thou comest to me with a sword, and with a spear, and with a shield: but I come to thee in the name of the Lord of hosts, the God of the armies of Israel, whom thou hast defied.
1 Samuel 17:45

King David was a mighty warrior. A king known for strength and courage. David is another character that was chosen at a young age. Seems like God always chooses the less likely ones to lead or to fight against the strongest armies. David was a keeper of the sheep before he was anointed to be king. God doesn't waste any of your experiences. Every part of your life plays a bigger role in the grander picture. In this particular story we see David has not yet stepped into his kingship. Even though he was anointed by Samuel the prophet he remained a shepherd boy for several more years. There are always pivotal points in each of our lives. This day would make history where a boy became a man. He would kill a giant with a sling and a stone. He would remember the past victories. David knew there was a strength beyond his human strength. He slew that giant in the name of the Lord. When God has appointed you in a certain place and time, you will have the courage you need to fulfill that call. Your destiny awaits.

Prayer (speak aloud)

God, I don't have a literal Goliath threatening me. I definitely can not use a sling. I have the enemy of my soul trying to steal, kill, and destroy everything that God has called me to do. The spirit of fear and torment shouts so loud sometimes I can't hear You speaking to me. I fumbled the ball many times on this journey called life. I know, like David, I have been anointed to slay giants. I can't fight this unseen enemy in my own ability. I come each time leaning on You, expecting to be covered with the armor of God. I am clothed with courage, not of my own but the courage that can only come from You. I will slay the giants. I will tear down the walls. I will speak to the mountain all in the name of Jesus. Amen.

**Did you feel a call on your life at a young age?
If not, what do you feel now?
Write down some giants that keep you stuck.**

Day 6

And, behold, a woman, which was diseased with an issue of blood twelve years, came behind him, and touched the hem of his garment.

Matthew 9:20

Courage was definitely present in this story. Though her name was not mentioned, her courage to press through the crowd that day is still one of the greatest events that took place in the Bible. This unnamed woman was not even supposed to be among people, let alone a crowd. We often hear that desperation calls for desperate actions. In biblical times a woman was to keep to herself if she was menstruating. Apparently this had become a serious problem. She couldn't seem to stop and became extremely ill. She said enough is enough. She said within herself if I could but touch the hem of His garment I know I will be made whole. Her story is often used in faith messages about speaking what you see in your spirit. Today we are sharing the courage it took to come out among the crowd knowing that if she was recognized it could mean sudden death for her. She didn't care anymore, she was going to die anyway if she couldn't get this problem to stop. She stepped out in courage that day and was made whole. Thank God Jesus has come and made it possible that we can all go to the throne no matter our circumstances.

Prayer (speak aloud)

Heavenly Father, I thank You for Your healing power. Thank You for the examples in Your Word, that if I need healing I can touch the hem of Your garment. I know that You no longer walk the earth in a fleshly body. You no longer walk down my street. I no longer can touch a real garment. You gave me the Word. It is my medicine. Thank You for the courage to believe in the healing power. I will find healing scriptures and stand on them. I will be bold and courageous. I may not have a death sentence on my life, but I need You everyday. I need courage to hold on until my help comes. I need courage to believe that You will make me whole, in Jesus' name. Amen.

**What do you think moved Jesus the most that day?
Have you ever felt desperate about a situation?
Do you have the courage to take chances and move
beyond the norm?**

_____
_____
_____
_____
_____
_____
_____
_____
_____
_____
_____
_____
_____
_____
_____
_____
_____
_____
_____
_____
_____
_____

Day 7

Now when Daniel knew that the writing was signed, he went into his house; and his windows being open in his chamber toward Jerusalem, he kneeled upon his knees three times a day, and prayed, and gave thanks before his God, as he did aforetime.

Daniel 6:10

I feel like the courage that Daniel is able display has to do with his consistency of praying. Three times a day. Windows open. On his knees, as he did aforetime. The only thing that they could find fault with was the way Daniel served God. It's really a witness for us today to have a strong prayer life. We know that a decree had been signed that anyone caught praying to any other God would be cast into a den of lions. This is courage on the highest level. Daniel did not stop praying. The aforetime without a doubt removed all fear. Could we be found guilty of praying too much? Could we have the courage Daniel had even after the decree was made? Honestly I don't know how I would respond. We will probably never be threatened by a lion's den. But we can learn from Daniel's example. When different situations try to overwhelm us and try to cause us to be fearful we can stand up and say we have done our due diligence. Daniel was thrown into the lion's den. He arose the next morning alive and unharmed. That my dear reader is being courageous.

Prayer (speak aloud)

God, I may never get thrown in a Lion's den. I may never have a decree signed against my praying. I want the courage that Daniel had. I definitely want to obtain the consistency of his prayer life. You will not make me pray. You will not make me fast. You will not make me do right. You simply gave me the Bible to lead and guide me. I will have to do my part to see the courage that I want to see in my life. I am not Daniel. But I am Your child and Your plans for me far exceed anything my mind can comprehend. Give me the courage to be a light in this world of darkness. Give me courage to be different in this world of conformity. Give me courage to discipline myself in any area that I need to move up in. Amen.

What do you think you would do if you were threatened like Daniel? Write about your prayer time. Would you improve it?

Day 8

But if not, be it known unto thee, O king, that we will not serve thy gods, nor worship the golden image which thou hast set up.

Daniel 3:18

We just shared the story of Daniel and the lion's den. Today we will share the story of his three friends that refused to bow to the golden image or worship other Gods. This was not the only time that the three Hebrew boys had been courageous. They also would not eat the king's meat. They chose to eat something like oats to show that the God they served would keep them no matter the situation. Daniel and the three Hebrew boys had to go through what they were threatened with. Daniel did go in the lion's den. Shadrach, Meshach, and Abednego were thrown into the furnace. It seems like their outcome was not sure. Yet, they were secure in their decision to not betray the true living God. We can Bee courageous today no matter what Satan throws at us. We will not eat the king's meat (compromise our biblical values) nor bow to this world's system and fear mongering. We may face some battles. We may see heartaches. But the God we serve will deliver us one day from this fallen world and set us in our rightful place.

Prayer (speak aloud)

O God, keep me from the attacks of Satan, keep me from the lies of those who want me to be afraid. Help me to be courageous in a world full of fear. Help me to not bend or bow to this world's economy. Help me see any possible trap that Satan has set up for me. I will not be persuaded by what I see with my eyes. I will stand on the Word in the midst of the fiery furnace. You will never leave me nor forsake me. You will always be the fourth man in the fire. I know Satan rears his ugly head in every situation. He tries to put fear in my heart. You said fear not over and over throughout Your Word. You said You have not given me the spirit of fear, but of love and a sound mind. Amen.

**Have you ever felt like you were in a fiery furnace?
How did God show up for you?
Write about a few times that God was the fourth man in the fire.**

Day 9

Now the L<small>ORD</small> had said unto Abram, Get thee out of thy country, and from thy kindred, and from thy father's house, unto a land that I will shew thee.
Genesis 12:1

Abraham (Abram) is another great example of courage. He comes on the scene in Genesis chapter 11. There is not a lot of story behind him before he gets this great command to leave his country and kindred. Though he is married to Sarah, he is still childless. Abraham is 75 years old and no child, yet God tells him He will bless his seed in this new land. God speaks into Abraham's life about his future. He tells him he will be a great nation. He will bless him and make his name great. We can assume there had to be some history between God and Abraham. We as humans don't like change for the most part. We definitely don't like the unknown. Could you just get up and go at the prompting of God? Could you leave your kindred and all the familiarity of your life? Everything God was telling him was future prophecy. Yet with no idea of the exact location Abraham obeyed what God told him. Abraham would need courage many times on his journey to destiny. Let's draw courage from Abraham's journey. He may not have known the total outcome but he trusted God.

Prayer (speak aloud)

Here am I, send me. God I say that so easily in this journal. I pray for the courage that I need to carry out my call in my own life. I want to be like Abraham and not question your instructions. I pray for strength to stand for You no matter where You lead me. I am not Abraham, but I am Your servant, I want to obey You. I will not allow fear to stop me from obeying Your voice. My seed will be blessed upon this earth, spiritually and naturally. I decree and declare today that I will let courage be my guide. I will not be afraid of my future. The stories that You purposely put in the Bible are my compass here on earth. I will build up my courage by reading about others that walked out their callings by prayer and faith in the unseen. Amen.

Have you ever moved away from your family? Did God call you to another place? Maybe you just moved because of a job or other life circumstance. Put yourself in Abraham's place today and share your own thoughts or even fears that you might have.

_____
_____
_____
_____
_____
_____
_____
_____
_____
_____
_____
_____
_____
_____
_____
_____
_____
_____
_____
_____
_____
_____
_____
_____
_____

Day 10

And Peter answered him and said, Lord, if it be thou, bid me come unto thee on the water. And he said, Come. And when Peter was come down out of the ship, he walked on the water, to go to Jesus.

Matthew 14:28–29

He walked on the water. Most of the time when someone is ministering from this passage they focus on the storm. How when Peter saw the waves he began to sink. While that is true, let's not forget he walked on the water. Also when they reentered ship they entered it together. I believe he started to sink but when Jesus got him by the hand He pulled him back up and they walked on the water back to the ship. Verse 32 says the wind ceased when they came onto the ship. The courage it took for Peter to step out on the water is a whole other level of courage. Notice he stepped out while the wind was boisterous. We are quick to step out of the boat (our comfort zone) when everything looks calm. He walked on the water. He had the courage to step out of the boat. Yes he began to sink when he took his eyes off Jesus. But when he cried out, Jesus caught him and they went in the boat together. We are all on a boat, the ship of Zion. We have all been called out to walk on the water. To step out of our safe places. I encourage you today, Bee courageous and walk on water.

Prayer (speak aloud)

Thank You God for reaching out your hand through Jesus time and time again. Thank You for calling me out of the boat. For showing me that You are with me at all times. Sometimes I see the waves and feel the wind while I'm navigating through my daily tasks. I am strengthened through these stories of courage. Many of Your followers were brave and journeyed into unfamiliar territory. I want to be the Peter of my day. I want to step out while others are not sure, or even afraid. I see the darkness, but I am the light. I see the chaos, but I am the calm. I feel fear sometimes when I am walking by faith. I walk by faith and not by sight. You are the lamp unto my feet, the light unto my path. I will be courageous as You hold my hand in the midst of the storm. Amen.

Did you ever focus on the part that Peter walked on the water? Have you ever noticed that he didn't sink? I love that they came into the ship together. Write about a time that you stepped out of the boat. What was it like?

_____
_____
_____
_____
_____
_____
_____
_____
_____
_____
_____
_____
_____
_____
_____
_____
_____
_____
_____
_____
_____
_____
_____
_____
_____

PART 2: CONFIDENT

Day 11

**8 It is better to trust in the Lord than to put confidence in man.
9 It is better to trust in the Lord than to put confidence in princes.**

Psalm 118:8–9

I chose these two scriptures for our first reflection in being confident because the number one person we need to put our confidence in is the Lord. Confidence in our own selves is also important, but we'll get to that later. In a world that is full of confusion, lies, and deceit we need someone we can have total confidence in with no reservations. We all know this to be the Lord. People will fail you. They will let you down. The Lord will never fail you. Even if trials come, even if His answer is no sometimes, the Lord will never leave you. Prayer will be the greatest tool in learning who you can trust. In verse 9 it even says princes, (a.k.a. leaders). We have to be able to discern the people who come into our lives, some just come for a little while, some will be lifelong friends. Never make a quick decision without trying the spirit. Always seek God first and know your trust is safe in Him. There may be people in your life who have walked with you through trying times. They are probably ones who put their trust in God as well. I don't want to come off in this reflection that you can only have confidence in God. My intention is to make you aware that people will take advantage of you, yet not all people are out to deceive you. Put total trust and confidence in the Word of God and always pray about any new opportunities.

Prayer (speak aloud)

Dear Lord, my trust and confidence is in You. I will seek You before moving forward in any relationship. My eyes are on You. I will not fear the unknown. Help me to know when to stay and when to walk away. Help me not to be anxious as I journey on the path that You have put before me. Bring the right people at the right time. Sharpen my spiritual antenna to know if someone can be trusted. Help me not be fearful as I move forward in life. I want You to be able to have confidence in me. Trust me to make the right decisions. I want to trust my walk with You. Hold my hand dear Lord and guide me on the right path. Amen.

Have you ever been deceived? I know I have. It makes it hard to put confidence in others.
Write some signs that you look for before moving forward with other people.

Day 12

I can do all things through Christ which strengtheneth me.

Philippians 4:13

Talk about a scripture that is power-packed with confidence, this is it. *All things* is such a strong statement. We see no lack in this verse. We see no fear. Christ is our strength. We can step out on nothing when we stand on this biblical truth. We must understand though that we have to have a personal relationship with Jesus to be able to speak this truth. We can't just just live any ole way and expect Christ to come through for us. There are guidelines and instructions all throughout the Bible that teach us the right way to conduct our lives. The verses before 13 are good examples. They tell us not to worry, not to fret. We are to be thankful and pray always. We are to think on things that are pure, just, lovely, honest, of a good report. Paul had a lot under his belt before he gave us this decree. He learned how to be content no matter the circumstance. When we have fought a good fight and when we have put God at the top of our list then we can say with great confidence that we can do <u>all things</u> through Christ.

Prayer (speak aloud)

Thank You, God, for the Apostle Paul that gave these simple but powerful decrees. I can be confident in all things. I can write books. I can build a business. I can do all things through Jesus Christ who gives me strength. I will think on things that are noble and true. Your Word is my road map. It points me in the right direction. No river is too wide. No mountain is too high. No valley is too low that I can't make it. Your strength is my crutch. The peace that I find in You is indescribable. With You by my side there is nothing I can't conquer. My confidence is strong. My heart is perfect toward the things of God. Amen.

**What would you do if you knew you couldn't fail?
Is your confidence strong in the Lord?
Do you see yourself as a confident person? Why or why not?**

Day 13

In the fear of the Lord is strong confidence: and his children shall have a place of refuge.

Proverbs 14:26

When we revere God and fear Him with a holy fear, we can walk in confidence. We can feel secure in our walk with God. We can be all God wants us to be. There is nothing that can stop us. Confidence should be a quality that all Christians have. If we lack it then it will show in our walk with God. We are to be a light in a world of darkness; this means sometimes we will have to move out of our comfort zone. We don't have to shun the sinner, we can simply show the confidence we have in God and share the good news of Christ. I like how this verse uses strong confidence. With strong confidence we can rest assured that a place of refuge is in our story. We can move forward in any situation that may come into our life. Many heartaches and uncertainties lurk around the corners in our journey. God promises to never leave us nor forsake us. That should give us the strong confidence we need. Sometimes we simply need to believe what the Word says about us, then we could be more confident about the next step we take.

Prayer (speak aloud)

Thank You, God, for teaching me to have the confidence I need to obey the callings You have placed in my life. I know that You are for me and You won't forsake me in my weakness. You are my refuge and strength. Your promises give me the confidence that I need to face each day without fear or doubt. I know that You dwell in me. I can do all things through Christ who strengthens me. Like David I can run through a troop and leap over a wall. You call me to step out on nothing and land on faith. Faith that doesn't waver. Faith that is strong. Faith that will help me to be confident in every area of ministry. Whether I'm ministering to one person or a group, there is a Holy confidence that rises up in my spirit when I have applied myself to Your Word. Amen.

What is one area that you have strong confidence in? Do you write? Do you speak sometimes to groups? What are your strengths? What do you shy away from?

_____
_____
_____
_____
_____
_____
_____
_____
_____
_____
_____
_____
_____
_____
_____
_____
_____
_____
_____
_____
_____
_____
_____
_____
_____
_____

Day 14

35 Cast not away therefore your confidence, which hath great recompence of reward. 36 For ye have need of patience, that, after ye have done the will of God, ye might receive the promise.

Hebrews 10:35–36

Confidence is almost like another form of faith. It is so important that God tells us not to cast it away. Great rewards come with having confidence. We can be calm while others are in chaos. We can lay down at night and sleep in peace. We can stand while others are stumbling. Why? Because our confidence is in the Lord. We have been patient. We have obeyed the Bible. We have received His promises. We can see how important our confidence is. We realize that we are nothing without God, but our relationship with Him gives us a certain stance in this world. We can trust that God will meet every need. Heal every sickness. Bring the finances we desire. Our confidence will be the light that shines in the darkness. It will speak in the midst of a storm without a word being uttered. Let us not cast our confidence away no matter what is going on in our lives.

Prayer (speak aloud)

God, I thank You for Your Word. I can decree it. I can declare it. It will not return void. The trust, the faith and the confidence I have is because You always make a way for me. Sometimes I may have to wait and be patient for the promises. As the snow and the rain comes down from above and waters the valleys and makes the flowers bud so is Your Word when it goes forth out of my mouth. That is why I have so much confidence in my walk with You. I have seen Your hand in my life in many ways. That is why I can stand with confidence today and everyday. You show up just in time. My God, that is who you are. Amen.

Can you remember the times that God came through just in time? Write about some of those on these couple pages. Let your spirit be encouraged.

Day 15

**11 According to the eternal purpose which he purposed in Christ Jesus our Lord:
12 In whom we have boldness and access with confidence by the faith of him.**

Ephesians 3:11–12

This whole chapter Paul is expressing his smallness in the kingdom. Yet, he understands that God is faithful and longs for His people to understand the teachings of the Gospel. Paul states that he is the least among the saints. Grace has been given to him to preach. Paul is sharing mysteries that have been hidden from the beginning. This is where he finds boldness and confidence in faith through God. We can boldly declare God's truth and revelations with confidence as well. The Word lets us know that the men and women in the Bible are just people like us. Sure it was a different era and time. Faith and confidence are things that we can live out in our day as well. Let's have confidence in what we preach and share. The Word of God will stand alone. It doesn't need to be defended. Because of Christ we can boldly declare the faith we have in our lives. Preach with boldness. Speak with confidence.

Prayer (speak aloud)

Thank You, God, for allowing me to walk in the same confidence and boldness that Paul walked in. I understand that it's not me that makes the difference. It is You. The life I live through You is my testimony. Everyday I look to You to guide my steps and give me the wisdom I need to make good decisions. I speak with confidence because of who You are. Because Your Word teaches me that You sing over me. You have called me from my mother's womb. Like Paul, I may have gone down the wrong path. Through Your Word all roads will lead me back home if I'm sincere about my walk with You. Your joy is my strength, and my confidence is true. My mind is made up to make it through. Amen.

Read the whole chapter of Eph 3. Write down what encourages you. Do you feel like Paul sometimes? Will you be confident in God's Word?

Day 16

5 Let your conversation be without covetousness; and be content with such things as ye have: for he hath said, I will never leave thee, nor forsake thee. 6 So that we may boldly say, The Lord is my helper, and I will not fear what man shall do unto me.

Hebrews 13:5–6

We can see confidence manifested in the truths that are being spoken in this passage. There is a contentment in God's call on our lives. We don't have to covet what others have. For he tells us He is our helper. He will never leave us nor forsake us. The word boldly shouts confidence to me. Being bold in these dark hours takes confidence. Not confidence in our own ability. Confidence in what God says about us and to us. In a world full of fear, we don't have to fear. In a world that lacks peace, we can have peace. When others seem lost and confused, we are secure and certain. How can we not be confident people with biblical truths like this to stand on? When we speak about God and His Word we are showing the world that we are confident in our walk with Him.

Prayer (speak aloud)

Thank You, Father, for a sure Word in these dark hours. I am content with the things that You have brought into my life. I can boldly proclaim Your Word because of scriptures like this. You are my helper and I will not fear what man can do unto me. Thank You for never leaving me nor forsaking me. Thank You for the food on my table and the clothes on my back. I never want to take that for granted. I have the confidence that what You began in me will come to fruition. That You will go before me and Your angels are all around me at all times. They are fighting against the devil for me. I know that I have no idea how many times You sent them to my rescue. My life is in Your hands, and my heart knows it. That is why I can have confidence in Your help. Amen.

Can you recall a few times that fear gripped your heart? Did it seem like God was far away? Will you believe His Word today that He will never leave you nor forsake you?

Day 17

14 And this is the confidence that we have in him, that, if we ask anything according to his will, he heareth us:
15 And we know that he hear us, whatsoever we ask, we know that we have the petitions that we desired of him.
1 John 5:14–15

What an encouraging word! Both of these scriptures are loaded. I'm happy that the word *confidence* is in these verses. Even if it wasn't, it's still a confidence builder. Finding God's will can seem daunting sometimes. Many of us struggle with that daily. We are all called to be Christ like, soul winners and witnesses. Each one of us has a purpose, though, something that sets us apart. That will be where we need confidence in our expectations from God. We watch others move seemingly easily in what God has called them to do. I can tell you, no doubt, they have questioned their purpose. What we all have to do is trust that God will lead us to the right place at the right time. We have to have confidence that God sees us and cares if we are walking out His will in our lives. Ask God to direct your steps. Ask Him to show you if you are going in the wrong direction. When we are sincere He is faithful to show us the way.

Prayer (speak aloud)

God, I ask You to help me to know Your will for my life. Help me not to be afraid to make a move. I have confidence in Your guidance. I ask today that You will move in my life. Open doors that will lead me to Your perfect will. I can not allow fear to keep me stalled. Whatsoever I ask according to Your will, I know that You hear me. Help me not to play the comparison game. Each one of us is gifted in different areas. I cannot belittle what I feel is important to me because of what others may think or even say. My flesh will want what it wants, but the Spirit will lead me to what I need. That is where I must put my trust in God and know that He will always have my best interest in His heart. I sincerely trust You, God, with all my heart and soul. Amen.

**Do you compare what you are doing to others?
Do you feel like you are praying amiss?
What is your action plan to not fall into this trap?
Write these verses out and let God speak to your heart.
Put your confidence in Him.**

Day 18

Being confident of this very thing, that he which hath begun a good work in you will perform it until the day of Jesus Christ.

Philippians 1:6

In this chapter, Paul is writing another letter to God's people. Paul often encourages his followers to hold on to what they have learned, to put their confidence in God, the maker of everything. God has a plan for our lives. It's not faulty. It's not lacking in any part. We as the children of God must do our best to follow after that plan. We don't always know the plan. Yet, the bible gives us plenty of examples to follow. We are to seek God and obey the Bible. When we do this, we are inviting God to order our steps. I love how Paul talks about how much confidence he has in the work God had begun in him. Not just a work, a good work. Then goes on to say God will perform it. If we will yield ourselves to God's plans, we won't fail. We should have the same confidence that God desires for us to succeed in the work He has called us to. After all He is our Father. He loves us with no strings attached. Remember, He started that work in you. You did not start it yourself.

Prayer (speak aloud)

Thank You, Heavenly Father, for the work You began in me. My confidence is strong in the Word. I ask you to lead me on the right path. I know that your plan for my life is perfect. You leave nothing unturned or any doubt that You are well able to perform what You started in me. Help me to not hinder my own progress. To seek Your ways and Your plan. Forgive me for the time I may have wasted running after my own plans, ignoring all the roadblocks in my spirit. Your ways are so much grander than mine. Your will for my life is what my heart longs for. Jeremiah 29:11 let's me know that You want me to fulfill the call in my life. The work You began in me will come to fruition. Because my confidence is in You. Not in myself or in anything else, just You. Amen.

**What work do you feel like God is calling you to?
Is your confidence strong in that area?
What area do you seem to feel insecure in?**

_____
_____
_____
_____
_____
_____
_____
_____
_____
_____
_____
_____
_____
_____
_____
_____
_____
_____
_____
_____
_____
_____

Day 19

2 When the wicked, even mine enemies and my foes, came upon me to eat up my flesh, they stumbled and fell.
3 Though an host should encamp against me, my heart shall not fear: though war should rise against me,in this I will be confident.

Psalm 27:2–3

David is confident that God will protect him. David had many enemies who desired to see him destroyed. Passages like this should help us stay strong and confident. We must realize that the enemies will come. Satan will bring out all his plots and schemes against us. He will use our families and our spouses. His favorite trick is to plant thoughts in our minds that someone doesn't like us, or our church family doesn't really care. The devil will use anything he can to throw us off our post of duty. We will begin to look around at the distractions, the other people in our lives and count them as our foes. We must know it's the devil at work. He is trying to rage war on your life. We must recognize that and put our confidence in the one true God. Satan's plots will stumble and fall when we know who we are in Christ and our rightful place in the kingdom. This confidence is only obtained through knowing the God you serve is well able to keep you in all circumstances.

Prayer (speak aloud)

My confidence is strong in You, God. It's not if my enemy comes, it's when he comes, he will not be able to cause me to fall. I will not fear. I will not back down. I have this confidence only because Your Word lets me know that You will fight for me. You will hide me under Your wings. You are my refuge and strength. Help me to see any blind spot or trap that Satan has planted in my path. Greater is He that is in me than he that is in the world. The gods of this world will never be able to defeat the God in me. It is You, oh God, that keeps my heart and mind through Christ Jesus. The enemy is defeated. And my life is hidden in Christ. Amen.

**What are some ways that Satan has tried to throw you off your game?
Do you fight from the knowledge that Satan is a defeated foe? God's Word says He will fight for you.**

Day 20

13 For thou hast possessed my reins: thou hast covered me in my mother's womb.
14 I will praise thee; for I am fearfully and wonderfully made: marvellous are thy works; and that my soul knoweth right well.

Psalm 139:13–14

When we need a boost of self-esteem, there is no better place to turn to than the Bible. When you feel like you're not good enough or strong enough, remember who God says you are. Scripture is filled with truths and promises that we can place our confidence in. This is one of those passages you can hang your hat on. It's a nail in a sure place. It's hard to comprehend that the God of the universe is concerned about our well being. That He cares about the smallest details. You can be confident of this one thing that God was there the second you were conceived. Verse 13 says He covered me in my mother's womb. He told Jeremiah that He called him from the womb. Each one of us has been born for a reason and a purpose. We were born at the right time for our assignment. Yes, we all have been born with an assignment. Satan desires to blind us of these truths that we are fearfully and wonderfully made. Our flesh may not grasp such intimate details, but our soul knows and longs for our Creator. This passage has confidence written all over it. Let God be the Author of your story, believe His Word and you will walk in confidence. You are not an accident.

Prayer (speak aloud)

When my heart is overwhelmed, Lord, help me to know that You are with me and for me. I may not understand how You watch over me. How You care about every detail of my life. All I know is my soul knows that I belong to You. Help me when I don't feel adequate enough to walk out the call in my life. Remind me of this passage when life seems too hard. Your Word tells me that my substance was not hidden from You. I was made in secret, and curiously wrought in the lowest part of the earth. Yet being unperfect, You wrote all my members in Thy book. You are the author finisher of my faith. I am confident. Amen.

**Does this passage make you feel confident?
Do you feel fearfully and wonderfully made?
Let's believe in His Word and move forward with confidence.**

_____
_____
_____
_____
_____
_____
_____
_____
_____
_____
_____
_____
_____
_____
_____
_____
_____
_____
_____
_____
_____
_____
_____
_____

PART 3: CONSISTENT

Day 21

Therefore, my beloved brethren, be ye stedfast, unmoveable, always abounding in the work of the Lord, forasmuch as ye know that your labour is not in vain in the Lord.

1 Corinthians 15:58

Consistency is key in any area of our lives. If we are going to move forward in our walk with God we must be consistent. This scripture tells us to be steadfast, unmoveable, always doing the right thing. When we remain consistent, our labor stays at the forefront of our endeavors. When we are steadfast, we are not easily detoured off of our path. Unmovable is such a strong word for our lives. Yet we can't be moved or persuaded every time we hit a bump in the road. Our actions must line up with our conversations. If we are unstable, it will show in our everyday life. We should seek God daily. We should pray and read the Bible daily. Not so we can check it off our list. We should do it for the reward that it brings into our walk with God. Labor doesn't mean relaxing. Work is usually involved. When we labor in love, we will feel content and fulfilled. Don't feel condemned for being slack. If there is an area you need to step up in, then make the decision to discipline yourself and find that consistency you need.

Prayer (speak aloud)

God, sometimes I don't measure up to Your desire for my life. I get slack and sometimes fall. Today I am declaring a new path for myself. I will be consistent in my Christian walk. Help me to be steadfast and unwavering. Let me labor with love and not dread. If I am consistent with my actions, then I know I will see a reward. I am planning on making heaven my home. I know that I will see Your goodness even while I live on this earth. Even when I stumble and make mistakes You are more than willing to forgive me and help me get back on track. Thank You, God, for Your consistent ways toward me. It helps me to realize I'm nothing without You. I pray this day for strength to stay on the right path. Amen.

What can you improve on today to help you stay consistent?
What area do you feel like you are slack in, if any?
What are your strengths in being consistent?

_____
_____
_____
_____
_____
_____
_____
_____
_____
_____
_____
_____
_____
_____
_____
_____
_____
_____
_____
_____
_____
_____

Day 22

Praying always with all prayer and supplication in the Spirit, and watching thereunto with all perseverance and supplication for all saints.

Ephesians 6:18

Praying always. With <u>all</u> perseverance. Being consistent. Like I said in the other reflection, we don't pray and read so we can check it off our to-do list. It's a discipline that we endeavor to keep at the forefront of our life with Christ. We won't always feel like doing it. We will feel disconnected sometimes. Our tendency is to go by our feelings. The Bible says when we have done all we know to do, stand therefore. If we have a consistent prayer life, the circumstances that surround our lives will not be able to throw us off our path. The more you pray, the more you long for that secret place. The more you will grow. The spirit man will get stronger. Satan's plots and schemes will be brought to light all because you stayed consistent in this area. Many things fight for our attention and our time. We must be diligent in blocking out that time. Sometimes life happens; trips, unexpected events, and even the death of loved ones can hinder that time. Get back to it ASAP. Consistent prayer is our lifeline to survive in this chaotic world.

Prayer (speak aloud)

God, I know that in my humanness I can get off course. I know that Satan wants me so busy that I can't find time to pray. He definitely doesn't want me to be consistent. Thank You for always reminding me to talk to You. Help me to block out a set time and stick to it. Help me to recognize the enemy's tricks. I know that my flesh doesn't always feel like praying. You are so merciful and kind to me, You bless me even though sometimes I'm slack in serving You. The more time I spend with You the more peace I have. I want people to know they can count on me to go to You on their behalf. To stand in the gap for them when they are heartbroken or just need You to move for them in some area. Prayer is key, and being consistent opens doors that only You can open. Amen.

**Do you have a specific time that you pray?
What are some things you have to do to make that happen?
Use these journal pages to write out a prayer!**

_____
_____
_____
_____
_____
_____
_____
_____
_____
_____
_____
_____
_____
_____
_____
_____
_____
_____
_____
_____
_____
_____
_____

Day 23

And be not conformed to this world: but be ye transformed by the renewing of your mind, that ye may prove what is that good, and acceptable, and perfect, will of God.

Romans 12:2

Renewing the mind is a powerful way to live a victorious life. How do we keep our minds renewed? Reading the Bible daily is one way. The more you read, the more you learn. When you study for a test, you read the material over and over. Some people will write it down several times. Writing down what is on the test helps us to remember as we take the test. Living for God and walking out our lives as Christians is compared to taking tests along the way. The more we study, the more likely we will pass this life's test. Again going back to taking tests at school, there is more than one test. There are many tests through one subject. Consistently renewing our minds through reading God's Word will keep us more aware of the enemy and his tactics. Scriptures like 'He will supply all my needs' will keep you when money is tight (Philippians 4:19). 'By His stripes we are healed,' will encourage you when sickness comes (Isaiah 53:5). Faith comes by knowing the Word. Be consistent brothers and sisters and grow, grow, grow.

Prayer (speak aloud)

Thank You, God, for the desire to keep my mind renewed. Your word tells me be not conformed to this world. You didn't leave us without instructions on how to perform this great task. Everyday is new opportunity to renew our minds. I pray to see things the way You see them. I pray to have the same compassion that You offer to the world. I pray to be strong and stand against the devil's darts. Thank You that Your Word has been my shield many times. You are consistent in loving me. You are consistent in helping me. Why would I not be consistent in renewing my mind? Through Your Word I have learned that I can stand in the midst of the storm. I can live a life of triumph through this simple yet profound act. Amen.

**What does renewing your mind mean to you?
Write out some of your favorite verses.
Rewrite them a couple of times, like studying for a test.**

Day 24

But let your communication be, Yea, yea; Nay, nay: for whatsoever is more than these cometh of evil.

Matthew 5:37

This scripture can be a hard pill to swallow. We have to be consistent with our words. We say one thing today and something different tomorrow. Did you know that most people will judge you by your words? Do you keep your word? Can people count on you to show up when you said you would? We can go so many ways with this. Parents, bosses, and pastors. Even husbands and wives. We must be consistent with our communication. The Bible says that if your ways, your conversations are not consistent it can become evil. We could easily find ourselves in the lying category. We all know a few people who are inconsistent with their words. We are fruit inspectors. We are not to mistreat or talk about them. We are to pray for them. We don't have to do business with them. God clearly wants us to be consistent. We should do what we say we are going to do. If something causes us not to be able to fulfill our commitment, then we should let the person know and not just leave it to chance. Let us not be easily persuaded to ignore our convictions. If we say no, then let it be no. If we say yes, then let it be yes.

Prayer (speak aloud)

Lord, I will be consistent with my words. If I say yes, then I will do all I can to fulfill that commitment. Help me as a parent to be consistent with what I teach every day. Help me to be the spouse that is consistent with love and grace. Death and life are in the power of my tongue. I can kill my influence by not being what I say that I am. I can cause other people to stumble because I'm not faithful with my actions. Thank You for teaching me how to be a person of my word. I can clearly see why the inconsistency of my communication could lead to evil. Help me, Holy Spirit, to be a spouse/person who is true to what I say. Not only my words but my actions as well. Thank you that my spouse enjoys coming home each day. They know they will find peace in our home. They will find consistency in my words. Amen.

**Does this scripture check your spirit?
Are you a person of your word?
What areas do you need to work on, if any?**

_____
_____
_____
_____
_____
_____
_____
_____
_____
_____
_____
_____
_____
_____
_____
_____
_____
_____
_____
_____
_____
_____
_____

Day 25

Wherefore the king said unto me, Why is thy countenance sad, seeing thou art not sick? this is nothing else but sorrow of heart. Then I was very sore afraid.

Nehemiah 2:2

The story of Nehemiah is a great example of being a consistent person. Apparently, Nehemiah was a happy person. He came before the king daily. He was so consistent with his words and actions that the king recognized it when it changed. We should find our flow and be consistent in it. I love the story of Nehemiah because in his time with the king he built a strong relationship. So much so that when Nehemiah longed to go rebuild the walls of Jerusalem the king granted him leave. Not only was he excused to go, the king sent letters with him to obtain the material he would need to finish the job. Nehemiah had favor with the king. Favor is usually acquired from being consistent with your actions and your words. Nehemiah's consistency didn't just pay off with the earthly king. He had favor with God as well. There may not be details of what all he did or was, yet we can read between the lines there was consistency in his life. We know that in 52 days, the walls were rebuilt, and he succeeded in his goal.

Prayer (speak aloud)

God, I long for favor from You. I want to be so consistent that when something is off or my heart is heavy, Your people will recognize it. That people like the king will be ready to help me in any way they can. I see it pays to be the same. To always put my best foot forward. I want people to feel like they can trust me and depend on me. God, it's through your word that I have learned how to be a person of integrity. You didn't leave us without a remedy. I will be the same every day. I will be consistent with my walk with You. All I have to do is ask You to move in a situation, You're all ears. You will send angels before me to work on my behalf. You will speak in people's heart about things concerning me. You will let me find favor in the eyes of man. Amen.

**Have you ever needed God to show favor on your behalf?
Do you consider yourself a consistent person?
Write about a time when your consistency paid off.**

Day 26

20 My son, attend to my words; incline thine ear unto my sayings.
21 Let them not depart from thine eyes; keep them in the midst of thine heart.
22 For they are life unto those that find them, and health to all their flesh.

Proverbs 4:20–22

Reading the Word of God is vital to our existence. Listening to teaching and preaching and reading Bible-based books are good for the soul. The more you do it the more it gets in your heart. We need it to be like coffee, tea, or sodas, or good food in general. If we don't have these we will start to feel ill or just plain hungry. Maybe you have a favorite food you eat almost daily. Everyone has different tastes and no one person is like the other. That is the way God made us. The Word of God will work for all of us the same though. We may hear it different ways, different times, even different versions. What it does though is the same. It will strengthen you. It will encourage you. It will teach you the ways of God. The number one way for most people to consume the Word is through reading it. Set a reminder on your phone if that helps you. When you keep it before your eyes and in your heart it will become a well of living water springing up inside you. You will be able to give others a drink in their draught season. The Word is health to all our flesh. We need to be consistent in our pursuit of learning more of the Word.

Prayer (speak aloud)

Thank You, Heavenly Father, for Your life-giving Word. Your Word is spirit and life. It heals. It is forgiving. It leads. Wisdom and knowledge is rooted in it. I'm never without an answer if I just simply read the instructions You put in the Bible. Thank you for all the different ways that I can receive Your Word. I am inexcusable to not be a winner in this life. The book of Proverbs is so full of life-giving substance. If I need strength it's in the Word. If I need finances it's in the Word. If I need healing it's in the Word. Whatever I have need of, it's in the Word of God. I will keep it before my eyes. I will put it in my heart. Amen.

What is your favorite way to get the Word in your heart? Do you read on your own or through a Bible app? Declare today that you will be consistent in consuming the Word.

_____
_____
_____
_____
_____
_____
_____
_____
_____
_____
_____
_____
_____
_____
_____
_____
_____
_____
_____
_____
_____
_____
_____

Day 27

7 In all things shewing thyself a pattern of good works: in doctrine shewing uncorruptness, gravity, sincerity,
8 Sound speech, that cannot be condemned; that he that is of the contrary part may be ashamed, having no evil thing to say of you.

Titus 2:7–8

When we are not consistent in our walk with God we leave the door open for the enemy to mar our reputation. It allows people to speak evil of you, and if you are known for being inconsistent you won't be able to defend the accusation. Let's not leave any room for him to work. Let's make sure that we have a pattern of good works. This helps to keep the devil from pushing his agenda. Sincerity, sound speech, and gravity, meaning no variableness in our walk. When people speak lies about us then our steadfastness and consistency will put them in their place, both the people and the lies. We won't get to heaven on good works alone, yet we do need to work. The Bible says that people will see our good works and glorify the Father. Good works can mean many things, maybe it's ministry or the work we do for money. No matter the job, big or small, we want everything we do to be consistent and reflect the goodness of the Lord. We need to work like the whole job depends on us and pray like it depends on God. These two actions coupled with consistency is a sure win in this journey we call life.

Prayer (speak aloud)

Remember me, God, for my good. Nehemiah prayed this prayer after he rebuilt the walls of Jerusalem. God, I thank You for leading me each day. Thank You for flowing through me to help other fellow Christians. I have learned that my Christian walk is made up of consistency, dedication, and good works. Teach me to number my days. Teach me to live like I will be gone tomorrow. I'm like a wave on the ocean, a flower in the field. Your Word teaches me the way I need to go. It teaches me how to love people well. I will be consistent in my walk with You. When others speak evil of me I will be able to have peace in my mind, because I know that I have done all You have asked me to do. Amen.

Name some good works/deeds you have done in your life. Are there some areas you want to be more consistent in? Ask God to show you who to bless this week and how.

Day 28

13 Who is a wise man and endued with knowledge among you? let him shew out of a good conversation his works with meekness of wisdom.
17 But the wisdom that is from above is first pure, then peaceable, gentle, and easy to be intreated, full of mercy and good fruits, without partiality, and without hypocrisy.
James 3:13, 17

We can add wisdom to our consistency. God is asking who is wise among you. Let it show forth through our conversation and yes good works. Having a consistent verbiage coupled with mercy and good fruits is a well balanced life. We can see throughout the Bible, it matters what you say and more so what you do. Let's face it, the age-old saying actions speak louder than words is definitely true. Wisdom is something that God intends us to grow in. Wisdom will help you to be the same person every day. There are wise people in this world who are millionaires because they know what to do and when to do it. How much greater should God's people be in this area? We can certainly be rich in the goodness of God. Our desire should be to show kindness, peace, and love with wisdom learned from the Bible. Without partiality, without hypocrisy, let us be consistent in how we treat people. The Word lets us know that everyone is different, which means people receive different. The wisdom comes by knowing how to speak consistently to each person where they are. God's wisdom is pure, peaceable, and gentle.

Prayer (speak aloud)

God, I ask for Your wisdom. Help me to show forth wisdom in my everyday life. Help me to be easily intreated. Let my words be consistent. Let my actions be consistent. All these things matter to You. It falls in my hands to study and seek Your ways. Thank You for showing me throughout scriptures that I can be wise as a serpent and harmless as a dove. Your Word teaches me how to be the same everyday no matter the circumstances. Help me to not allow the things that are going on around me to affect what my heart knows. Let me be a person of integrity. Help me to not have respect of persons because of worldly things. I want to be a drink to the thirsty. I want to speak a word in due season to they who are weary. I can only do that with Your help. Amen.

**What comes to your mind when you think of wisdom?
Do you feel like you are wise concerning people?
Are you consistent with your actions?**

Day 29

**2 And the things that thou hast heard of me among many witnesses, the same commit thou to faithful men, who shall be able to teach others also.
3 Thou therefore endure hardness, as a good soldier of Jesus Christ.**
2 Timothy 2:2–3

When we are faithful and consistent we become witnesses for the kingdom of God. We can teach others in words and deeds. The old saying that we are the only Bible that some people will ever read is so true. God wants us to take what we have heard and share it with others. When people see your consistency it is easy for them to learn from you. If we are up and down, in and out, how can we teach others? When we endure hardness it shows other people that it can be done. That they can learn from our actions, our walk with God. It's a great honor for God to entrust you to pour into other people's life. How do we gain this faithfulness? How do we become a person of value? Through being consistent. Yes, it is that simple. But it's not easy. We have to choose to do the right thing day in and day out. Do the right thing even when wrong is being done to you. That my friend is being a faithful follower of Christ. It gives your voice power to speak into situations and speak peace in the midst of chaos.

Prayer (speak aloud)

God, I am your faithful witness. I have endured hardness as a good soldier. I will teach others as You lead me. Thank You for helping me be a light in this dark world. Thank You for having confidence in my walk. That You trust me to speak into people's lives. I know that it is You who gives me the courage and wisdom to teach others. You are my strength when I'm weak. You are my wholeness when I feel broken. Help me to encourage others to be consistent, to be faithful, to be that teacher that they long to be. Help my witness be all it needs to be. When I speak, I release words into other people that they will receive them as from You. Amen.

Do you feel qualified to teach others? Yes or No?
Have other Christains spoken into your life?
Did you receive it well?

Day 30

And let us not be weary in well doing: for in due season we shall reap, if we faint not.

Galatians 6:9

Let's be honest, this verse though short in words can be the one of the hardest ones to live by. If You have lived for God any length of time you have stood on this verse. When we consistently do what is right and things seem to go wrong, we can grow weary. We will ask God how long is this going to last. We will wonder if it's worth it. Can I tell you it is. The Christian has five seasons. One of them being due season. Sometimes it feels like winter right in the middle of summer. Sometimes I'm weary on my journey. We can find comfort in His Word. When you have done all to stand, stand therefore. Keep standing. Keep believing. Keep asking, seeking, and knocking. There are more passages that we stand on. If God be for us who can be against us? The Bible is an inexhaustible book of wisdom and instruction on how to keep going. We will get weary sometimes with well doing. But, let us not stay in that place. Don't faint. Stay consistent in doing what is right. We will reap a good harvest. It will be worth it.

Prayer (speak aloud)

Oh Lord, this scripture is a great encouragement to me. I know that I grow weary doing well. Especially when the return is not so great. Help me to look beyond the now and see the future. Thank You for the due season. I will stay consistent in the face of adversity. Sowing and reaping is Your grace for doing what is right. I know that I have failed You in this area many times. Forgive me. Remind me of Your wisdom when I need to be reminded. I am forever grateful for the promises You have given me. I will keep doing what is right. I will keep sowing good seeds. I will reap in due season if I faint not. Amen.

**Is this a scripture you stand on when things are not going as planned?
Have you ever grown weary doing what is right, only to see the opposite?
Have you seen this verse come to pass in your life?**

Day 31

**Jesus Christ the same yesterday,
and to day, and for ever.**

Hebrews 13:8

I chose this verse last on purpose. We can count on Jesus to be the same everyday. We sometimes miss it because we are fleshly. I need this reminder daily. Our consistency can waver because of circumstances. That doesn't mean we have failed or we missed the mark. We just live in a broken world with broken people. We don't always get it right. But He does. That, my dear reader, is the greatest comfort we can have. He doesn't change. He doesn't waver. He is the same everyday, which means He is consistent. He will be there for us. He will not forsake us. His love for us held Him on the cross. He could have called 10,000 angels to come to His rescue. What a great comfort that Jesus doesn't change the way He feels about us because we miss it sometimes. He compares His actions toward us as parents do for their children. We as parents know how we long to make our children feel loved and cared for. We love to give to them. We want them to feel safe. I'm thankful for His consistency.

Prayer (speak aloud)

Thank You, God, for this promise. I can feel secure in standing on Your Word. Thank You for being a constant in my life. Thank You for being consistent. You're consistent in provision, healing, and miracles. You're the same everyday. I find it easier to get through each day knowing that you are with me at all times. I know that I can be inconsistent with my day to day life. I don't want to be, help me with that God. I want to be the person that the world needs. I want to be the Esther for my season. I love the fact that I can go to sleep tonight and in the morning You are not only there, You are still the same loving, caring, and forgiving God. Amen.

**How does that make you feel that Jesus is the same everyday?
What are some things that you can count on everyday from Jesus?
Thank God Jesus never changes.**

Why bees?

My series of Bee Devotionals was birthed out of a deep desire to have a ministry that would encourage, inspire, and pour into somebody else who wants to make a difference. Don't let what others say about you or even your own thinking limit a limitless God. The bumblebee shouldn't be able to fly because of the structure of its body, but it flies anyway. So can you.

Over the next few years, I'm hoping to develop a total of 12 "How to Be..." devotionals to inspire and encourage Christians who want more out of life. Recently, I set up my website, Beeministries.com, where you can find out more and read my blog. My YouTube channel for Bee Ministries offers devotional readings, sermons, heartfelt stories, and inspirational words. My first book, *Life After the Mistake*, is a creative nonfiction story about what it's like to be caught up in the sin of adultery. It's available on Amazon along with the Bee Devotional series and a short ebook I developed called *How to Bee a Writer*.

From the bottom of my heart, thank you for reading my book and taking the time to let God work within you through words. It changed me. And I believe it can change you too.

-Sheila

MORE BOOKS BY SHEILA TEXTOR

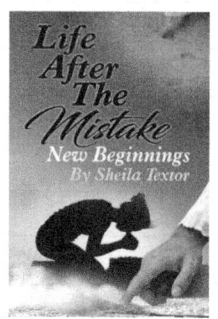

Introducing Victory

We have a new addition to the Bee Ministry family. We introduced her in the last devotional, *How to Believe in your Dreams*. Her name says it all, Victory. You will find her in this devotional being courageous, confident, and consistent. She exhibits a courageous pose on each day. Then she flys around the journaling pages to inspire you to believe in your future and to pour out your dreams and goals on those pages. So write like no one is watching and be all you can be in Christ Jesus.

FLY ANYWAY!!

NEED MORE SPACE TO JOURNAL?

ALL BOOKS AVAILABLE ON AMAZON

Made in the USA
Middletown, DE
15 November 2025